PYRAMID SCHEME

BY SALLY ODGERS
ILLUSTRATED BY NAHUM ZIERSCH

EDUCATORS PUBLISHING SERVICE
Cambridge and Toronto

© 2008 by School Specialty, Inc.

Series Authors: Kay Kovalevs and Alison Dewsbury
Commissioning Editors: Rachel Elliott, Tom Beran, Lynn Robbins, and Laura Woollett
Project managed by Rebecca Henson and Katherine Steward
Text by Sally Odgers
Illustrated by Nahum Ziersch
Edited by Emma Short
Designed by Justin Lim

Making Connections® program developed by School Specialty, Inc. and by
Pearson Australia (a division of Pearson Australia Group Pty Ltd).

ISBN 978 0 8388 3356 8

2013 2012 2011 2010
10 9 8 7 6 5 4 3 2

Printed in Dongguan City, Guang Dong Province, China, May 2010

CAST OF CHARACTERS

MATT
SMART AMERICAN
TEENAGER, VISITING
EGYPT

DAD
MATT'S BUSINESSMAN
FATHER

ALI
DAD'S BUSINESS
PARTNER IN CAIRO

TAMIR
ALI'S SON,
A PYRAMID GUIDE

AHMED
A GUARD AT
THE PYRAMID

SOUVENIR SELLER
AT 'RASHID'S REPLICAS'

He's wrong, I'm sure of it. Is he up to something or does he just not care?

MATT IS CERTAIN SOMETHING STRANGE IS GOING ON, BUT WHAT?

RASHID'S REPLICAS

I told you last time, I don't want fakes. You said you would have genuine—

SHID'S PLICAS

One moment, sir. Hello! Back again?

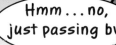

Hmm...no, just passing by.

THE NEXT MORNING, MATT STOPS AT RASHID'S REPLICAS TO INSPECT A SET OF CANOPIC JARS.

Yes, madam, this is very nice scarab. It's a great gift.

Right, a set of four jars. Falcon, jackal, human, and baboon heads.

Would you like to buy something today? I can sell you a full set of canopic jars at a special price. They are nice replicas.

Hmmm.

MATT LOOKS FOR A HIDING PLACE WHERE HE CAN SPEND THE NIGHT AND KEEP WATCH OVER THE CANOPIC JARS.

Tamir said this sarcophagus is empty. Maybe I can hide in here.

MATT CAREFULLY CLIMBS INTO THE SARCOPHAGUS.

There goes Ahmed. I hope he doesn't check in here!

MATT HAS BEEN WAITING FOR HOURS AND NOTHING INTERESTING HAS HAPPENED. HE IS TIRED OF THE CRAMPED HIDING PLACE.

Yawn...

SUDDENLY, AN INTRUDER ENTERS THE PYRAMID.

CLOMP
CLOMP
CLOMP

Uh-oh! Who's that?

FROM INSIDE THE SARCOPHAGUS, MATT WATCHES AS THE INTRUDER OPENS HIS BAG.

I've got to get his picture!

THE INTRUDER REMOVES A CANOPIC JAR FROM HIS BAG AND PLACES IT ON THE TABLE.

It's the missing jackal jar! But it looks new. He must be replacing the real jars with replicas, one at a time!

MATT TAKES A PHOTOGRAPH OF THE THIEF AS HE TAKES THE BABOON JAR.

Gasp!

CHA- CLICK.

Gotcha!

MATT REALIZES THAT HE MUST FIND THE POLICE.

Kids! Always in a hurry.

Slow down young man!

Oh no!

SOMEONE POINTS THE WAY TO THE POLICE STATION.

Just up this street.

Thanks!

MATT ARRIVES BACK AT ALI'S HOUSE. HE'S TIRED AND HIS LEGS HURT FROM BEING CRAMPED UP IN THE SARCOPHAGUS ALL NIGHT.

Matt! Where have you been?

It's okay, Dad. I'll explain everything.

Your son has helped us catch a criminal.

MATT TELLS HIS STORY.

Rashid, the owner of the souvenir stall, was replacing real canopic jars with replicas. Then he sold the real ones to 'special customers.'

And you discovered this on your own?

You have a smart son. He's very observant.

Pretty cool, dude.

I'm going back to the pyramid tomorrow. I want to see if the police got the real jars back. Do you want to check it out?

Definitely!